EATS

EATS

Poems by Arnold Adoff
illustrated by Susan Russo

Lothrop, Lee & Shepard Books
New York

Library of Congress Cataloging in Publication Data.   Adoff, Arnold.   Eats.
SUMMARY: Reflections on the poet's love of food and eating.   1. Food—Juvenile poetry.   [1. Food—Poetry.   2. American poetry]   I. Russo, Susan.   II. Title.
PZ8.3.A233Eat   811'.5'4   79-11300   ISBN 0-688-41901-1   ISBN 0-688-51901-6 lib. bdg.

Recipe For Eats Poems

Take One Grandma Ida in a warm kitchen smelling
     of Russian Coffee Cake and Gorky
add   One Mother Rita in a warm kitchen smelling
     of French Toast and Maupassant
combine
with One Wife Virginia
                 in a warm kitchen smelling
     of Plum Sauce and Gertrude Stein
season
with Two Children Jaime and Leigh
             in a warm kitchen smelling
     of Brown Bread and Milne
place
inside A Poet$_s$ head and cook for a long time
then
serve with the enthusiasm of An Editor Dorothy
        to hungry Readers ready for the taste

Eats

           are on my mind   from early morning
              to late at night
                                    in spring
                                    or winter
          there is
              no wrong
              or right
                  time
              to feel that sudden
                              need
              to find that sudden
                              meal

    i am always hungry

Not Me But

cows walk up and beg to
be
burgers
chicken legs
will tap dance
to
my
teeth
and
oatmeal cookies
have
been
known
to fly
out of their jars
as i pass by

My Mouth

stays shut
        but
food   just
finds
    a way

            my tongue says
we are
        full today
        but
            teeth just
                grin
        and
        say
            come in

i am always hungry

Love
Song

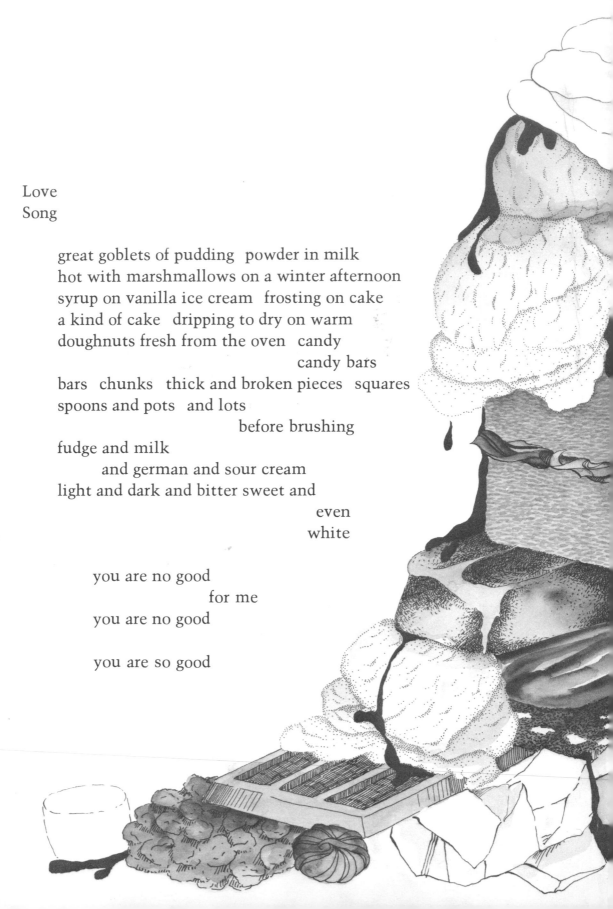

great goblets of pudding powder in milk
hot with marshmallows on a winter afternoon
syrup on vanilla ice cream frosting on cake
a kind of cake dripping to dry on warm
doughnuts fresh from the oven candy
                              candy bars
bars chunks thick and broken pieces squares
spoons and pots and lots
                        before brushing
fudge and milk
       and german and sour cream
light and dark and bitter sweet and
                              even
                              white

       you are no good
                   for me
       you are no good

       you are so good

Chocolate
Chocolate

       i
love
  you so
      i
want
   to
marry
   you
    and
live
  forever
     in the
      flavor
of your
  brown

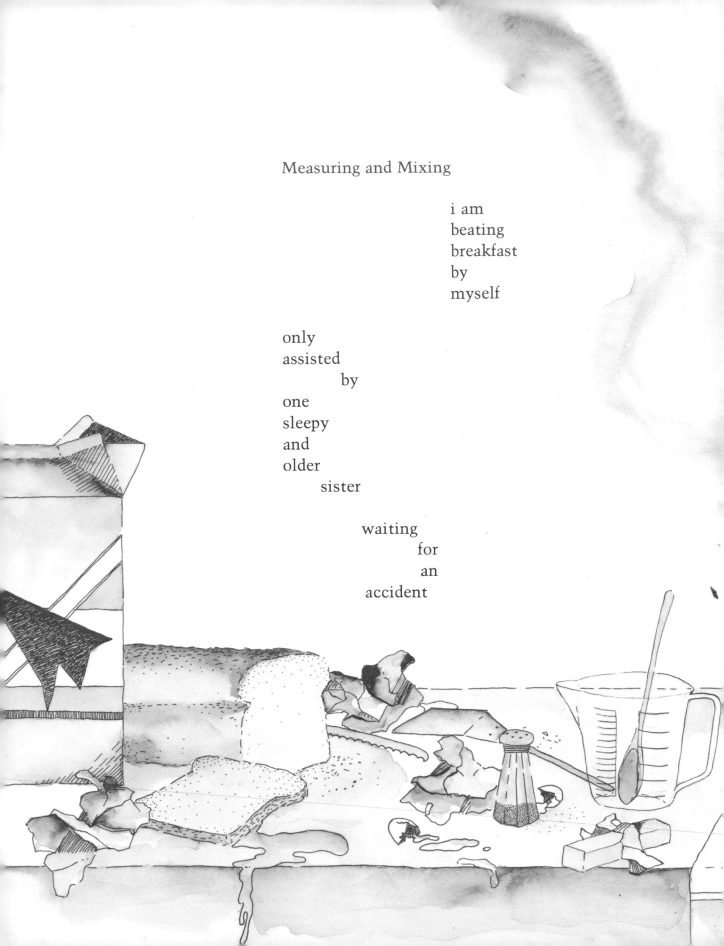

Measuring and Mixing

i am
beating
breakfast
by
myself

only
assisted
            by
one
sleepy
and
older
            sister

        waiting
                for
                an
        accident

As Long As

                    she helps
                          me
at the stove
                    with the
                         low
                       flame
my french
           toast
is   always
       better browning
                         in
                        the
           butter

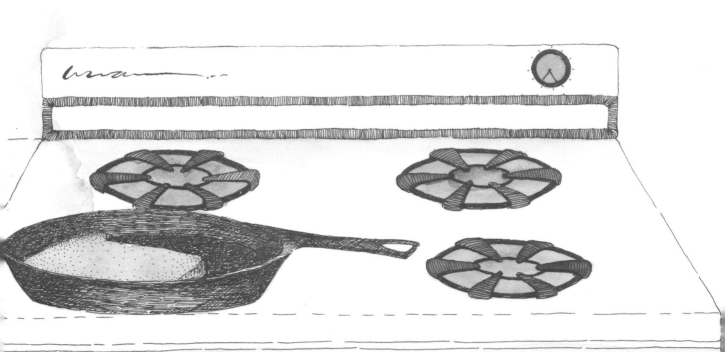

Sunday Morning Toast

                in a bowl   beat 2 eggs
                with ½ cup milk
                a pinch of salt
                ½ teaspoon vanilla

      dip 4 pieces of white bread   one at a time
            into this mix   and when the
                            bread
            is soaked through
             it is ready to go
    into
        a hot and buttered skillet
              or pan

then brown both sides until fluffy and done
and sprinkle with powdered sugar   or drip
                      honey
or maple syrup   then eat

makes enough to fill one sister and one cook
       and one sunday morning boast

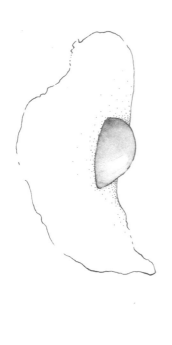

Sunny

    side
        up
    bull_s

    eye
    egg

    turn

    over
    easy
       and
    don_t bre_{ak}

    the
    yoke

Only The Onions

                                                    are first
even before
the
last frost   into the
                        ground
                    they
                        go

to grow
 a green
   fence around the
                    cabbage
    and the lettuce
    and the beans

they will keep
               the hungry
                 young
                 rabbits

                 out

After All The Digging

                              and the planting
                              and the   pulling
of weeds
            on hot summer afternoons

there are cool mornings
we can
            walk between
the rows
            and bite a bean   or chew a lettuce
                                          leaf
            and taste the ripe tomatoes
the
way
the rabbits
                take
    breakfast

Getting The Sweet

                         strawberries
from my
fingers
        down
        into the basket
without
        eating all of them
                            up
                            is
        the problem

        the solution
                    is
                  not
          to solve
          the problem
until
      you
        are
      full
          of answers

The Apple

                    is on the top
branch
          of the tree
                    touching
the
sky
          or the apple is
                    in
          the
          sky
touching
          the top branch
                    of the tree

and i am
          me on the ground
          waiting
                    for
                         a
          good
          wind

Take One Apple

                          wash and
                                dry
and
eat
   it   up and down
              and side
                   ways
to
the
core

           then
           take
                 one
                 apple
                 more

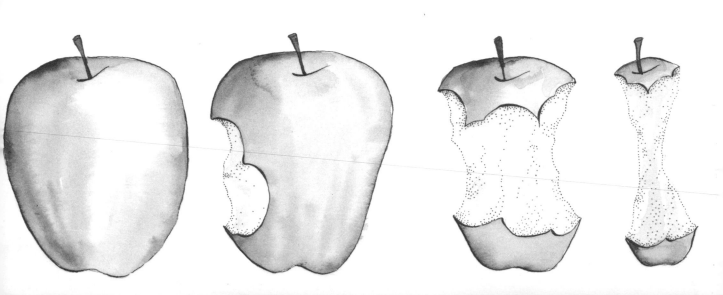

Take One

      old apple tree   and climb and shake
      and pick enough apples   to fill one
large
      grocery bag
            then carry them
                       inside
           and begin to work

cut out the core   of seeds
cut the apples in half
cut out the worms and bugs
                peel and slice
                   thin

then follow your best family recipe for pie
or cobbler or tarts or cake or crisp   or pic
or crunch or turnovers or dumplings or pie

get help on everything but the eating

At The End Of Summer

                              when the old tree   is full
                              and leaning to the ground
                              with its heavy load
i pledge my loyalty
                    to apple pie
                              and
i insist on deep
          done dough
as heavy as gold
as golden
          as sweet sun
                    and
                         no other
          of this
                    natural   world

unless
        there is a peach or rhubarb national
        emergency   or mince and pumpkin flooding
        in the fall   and the president calls
        to ask
                will you please do your share
                        and eat for dear america

        wild berry in the spring   chocolate
                cream   or boston dream and
                                        all
                the other flavors that
                                        wake
                me shaking in the night
                                        are
                only tasty second best

until
        each end of summer
                                when i pledge
        my loyalty again to
                        apple
only
        and always
                        apple

Grandma Ida_s Cookie Dough For Apple Pie Crust

mix in a large bowl   ½ cup sugar
                       ½ cup oil
                       2 eggs   until they are creamed

add   2 tablespoons orange juice
       ½ teaspoon vanilla   and stir well

sift together   2½ cups flour
                 2 teaspoons baking powder
                                      and
add this flour combination to the
creamy liquid   but do it slow   then stir until you have
                                      a soft ball of dough

cover with a kitchen towel and place in refrigerator
       from 2 to 12 hours   until you are ready for pie
then grease and flour a pan   spread out half of the dough
       ball until you have a bottom crust for your pie

or you can flour a board and roll out the dough to make
       two crusts   a bottom is a bottom   but a top can
       be strips of dough   or one whole crust

just   get your apples and begin

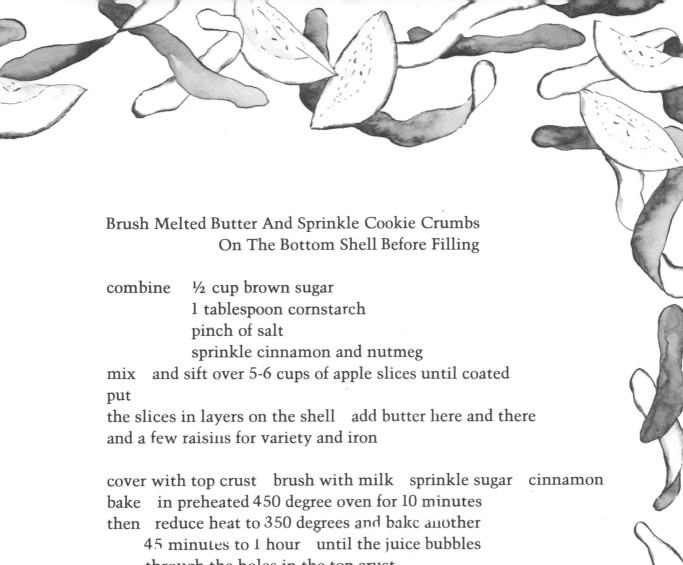

Brush Melted Butter And Sprinkle Cookie Crumbs
        On The Bottom Shell Before Filling

combine   ½ cup brown sugar
          1 tablespoon cornstarch
          pinch of salt
          sprinkle cinnamon and nutmeg
mix   and sift over 5-6 cups of apple slices until coated
put
the slices in layers on the shell   add butter here and there
and a few raisins for variety and iron

cover with top crust   brush with milk   sprinkle sugar   cinnamon
bake   in preheated 450 degree oven for 10 minutes
then   reduce heat to 350 degrees and bake another
       45 minutes to 1 hour   until the juice bubbles
      through the holes in the top crust
                         and the smell
o the smell

Thank You

         after the buds and the blossoms
        and the apples grown full of juice
     you
     can   on an august morning   after your
                  belly is full

    give the old tree a hug

Hard

is
in
  the
middle
   of
    a
carrot
  on
   a
loose

tooth

Soft

is
on
  a
  bed
with
book
a
pillow
for my
head
   and
quiet

Raisins
  in
   one
hand

Dinner Tonight

                        is hiding
in a mystery of steam
from
      the bowl of
spaghetti
              and meat sauce
              and
we
    must make our way through
    oregano fogs
                  and the deadly smog
              of a grated   cheese
                              breeze
      into a parmesan dream

past
    snapping beans and over broccoli logs
    we are in pizza country
        and there is danger
                            of
                            pepperoni
                            poisoning
        until dessert

The Baker

wanted me to know
that
underneath   the cheese
and
sausage bits
and
pepperoni
slices   and beneath the onions
and mushrooms and green
pepper
dices
the only thing that counted
was
the
dough

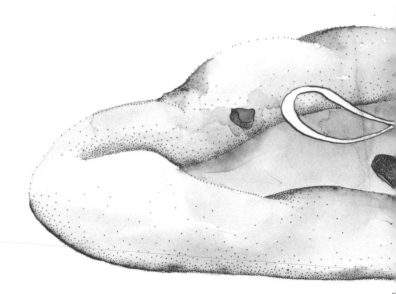

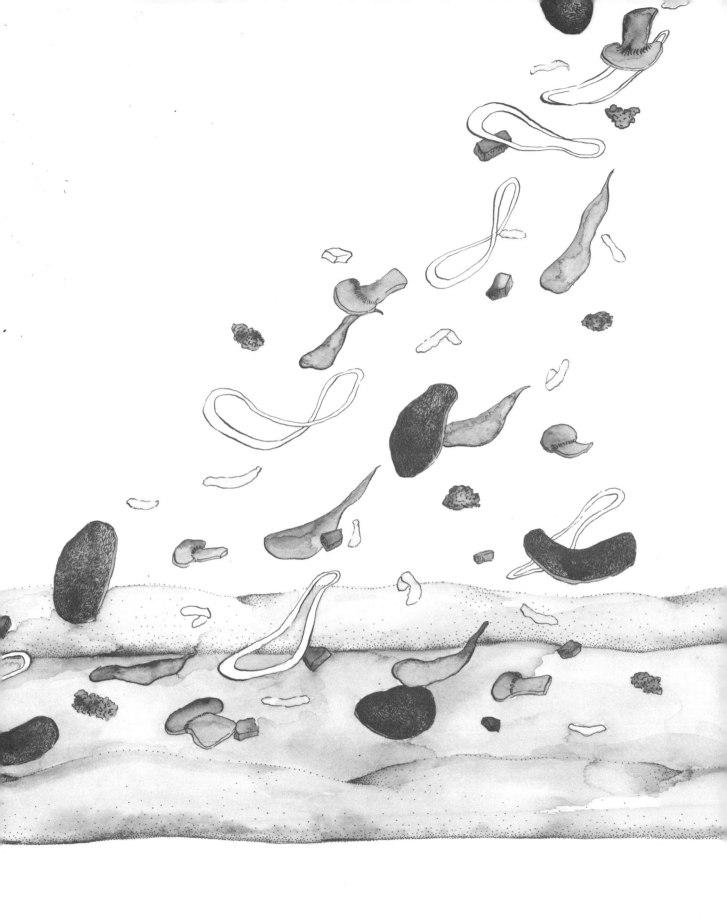

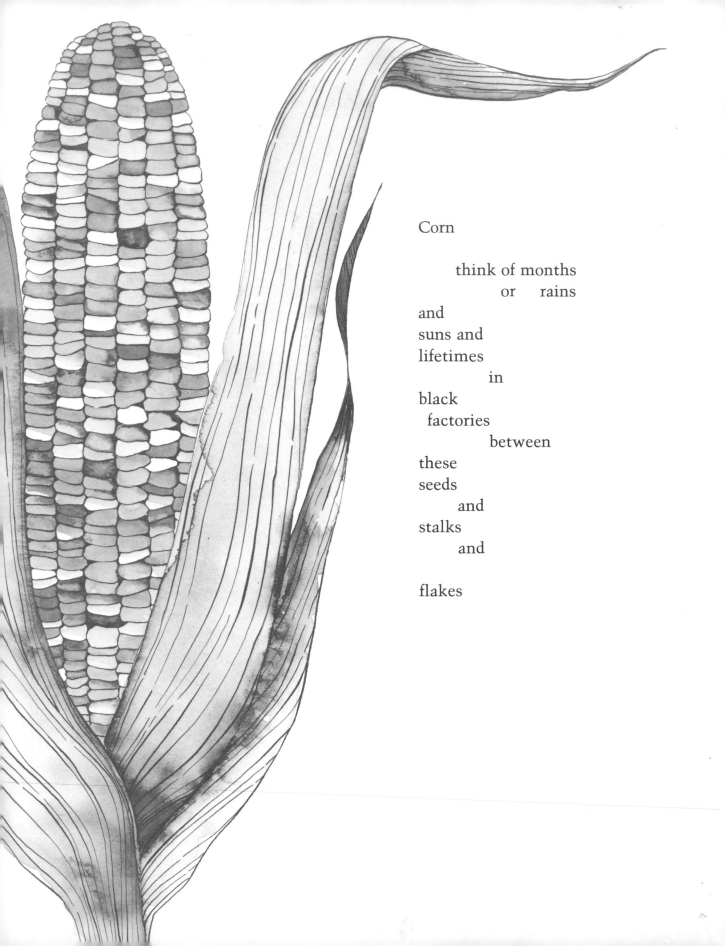

Corn

      think of months
              or   rains
and
suns and
lifetimes
          in
black
  factories
           between
these
seeds
      and
stalks
      and

flakes

Burger

      back

        up

seven

spaces

     into

       my

mouth

      do

      not

pass

      go

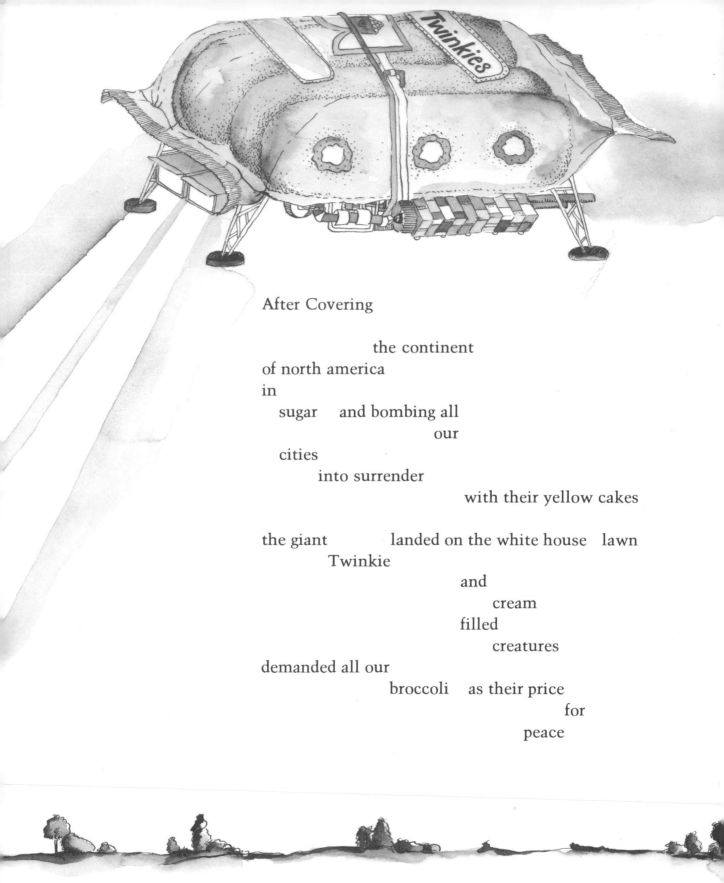

After Covering

        the continent
of north america
in
    sugar   and bombing all
                our
cities
     into surrender
              with their yellow cakes

the giant   landed on the white house lawn
      Twinkie
             and
            cream
         filled
           creatures
demanded all our
       broccoli as their price
               for
         peace

Sun Flowers

             they are so beautiful
in perfect
         circle
         rows
inside
        their collars of green
              leaves

       we hate to pick
           their seeds
                out
                 for
         the oven pan

they will roast
         slowly
and
dry   to the
           taste
      of autumn
sun

Cut
Out

an ugly face   with triangle eyes
and a big   tooth   mouth   for the
candle   glow
then scrape the seeds
out
and
wash them
and put them
in a flat and shallow
pan
in a low oven
for as long as you can wait
this dark night

when they are done baking
you
eat
be fore
booing

Under

      this autumn sky   i think of these
      ingredients when they were rooted
      in the ground
               that pound of flour
                       as
          some stalks
                 of wheat
    this sugar as
            sweet
          sugar canes or beets

          even the chicken eggs
         and salt and rising
                 yeast

i always use this wooden spoon to stir
             the batter for the bread
it was
     once a tree   or part of a tree
            rooted in the ground
under
    the
    sky

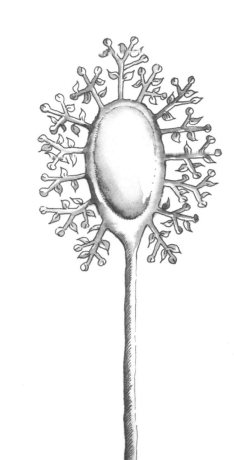

Turn The Oven On
           To 350 Degrees   and Grease
        A Deep And Round Baking Pan

first   combine in a large bowl   2 cups unsifted flour
                               2 envelopes dry yeast
                               1 tablespoon salt
                               ¼ cup sugar
then   heat in a small pot
                               1 cup milk
                               1 cup water
                               ¼ cup oil
until you have a warm liquid
        that is not too hot

        mix this warm liquid   and 2 eggs
              into the flour combination
blend
until the yeast is dissolved

use a wooden spoon to stir into the bowl
        another 2½ cups of flour
then keep stirring until you have a bowl
                of stiff batter

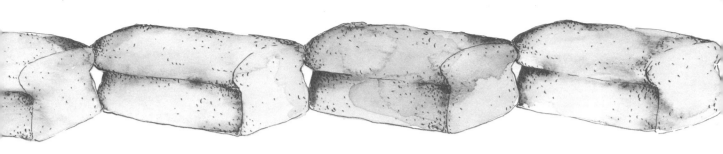

Cover The Bowl With A Kitchen Towel

put in a warm place   and let the dough rise
for an hour   then stick your wooden spoon
into the dough and stir it down   and spoon
                                    it into your pan

bake for 45 minutes   until the loaf begins to brown
then
take it out of the oven and brush on an Egg Wash or
                                        Dorure
                of   1 egg yolk
                            beaten with
                2 tablespoons of milk
                    and a pinch of salt

then
bake again until golden brown

            remove from oven

                        cool
                down

Good For The Head

                              when you need more
                                        sleep
but
you are sitting at the breakfast
        table
              instead
not
    ready for school

                              some quiet
                                    cream
                              of
                                    peanut
                                      butter
on a piece
              of
natural
        brown
          bread

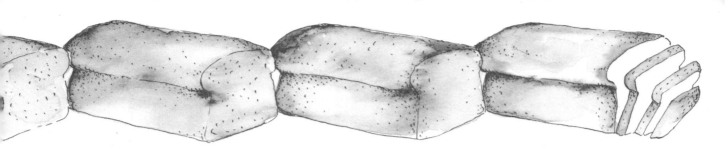

Peanut Butter Batter Bread

mix in a large bowl   1 cup unsifted flour
                              ½ cup instant oats
                              ½ cup yellow cornmeal
                              ½ cup sugar
                              ½ cup powdered milk
                              3 teaspoons baking powder
                              1 teaspoon salt

when they are all stirred together well
       add 2/3 cup peanut butter (either kind)
       and combine until the pieces are small
then
beat 2 eggs and 1½ cups milk (liquid)
       add to flour mixture   stir well
pour
into greased and floured 9x5x3 bread pan

bake in preheated 325 degree oven for an hour

remove   cool   spread   eat

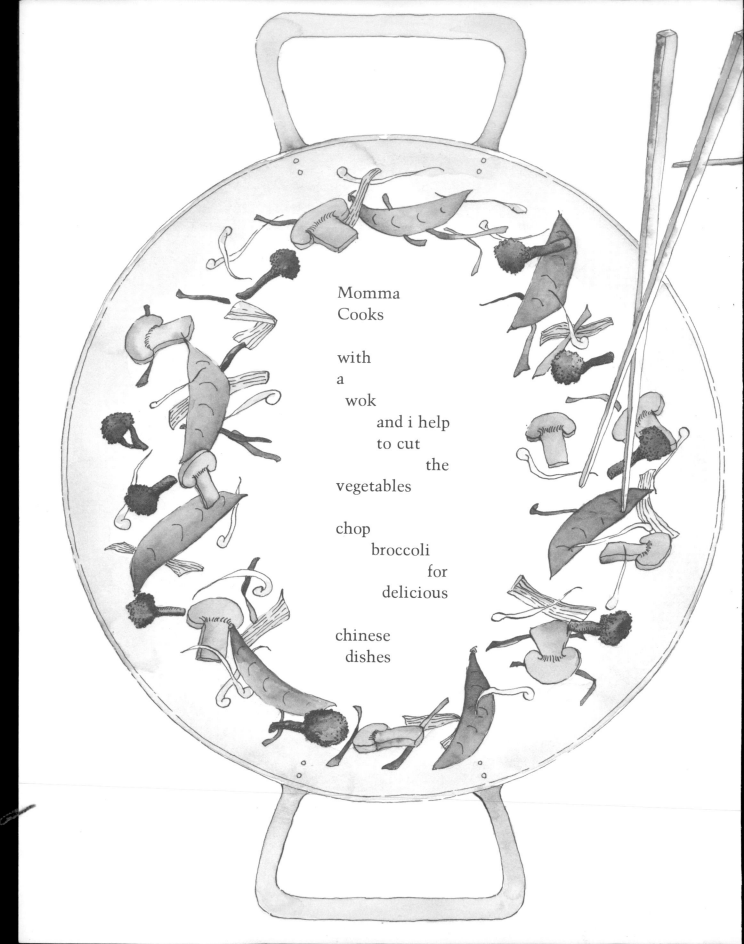

Momma
Cooks

with
a
    wok
        and i help
        to cut
                the
vegetables

chop
    broccoli
        for
        delicious

chinese
    dishes

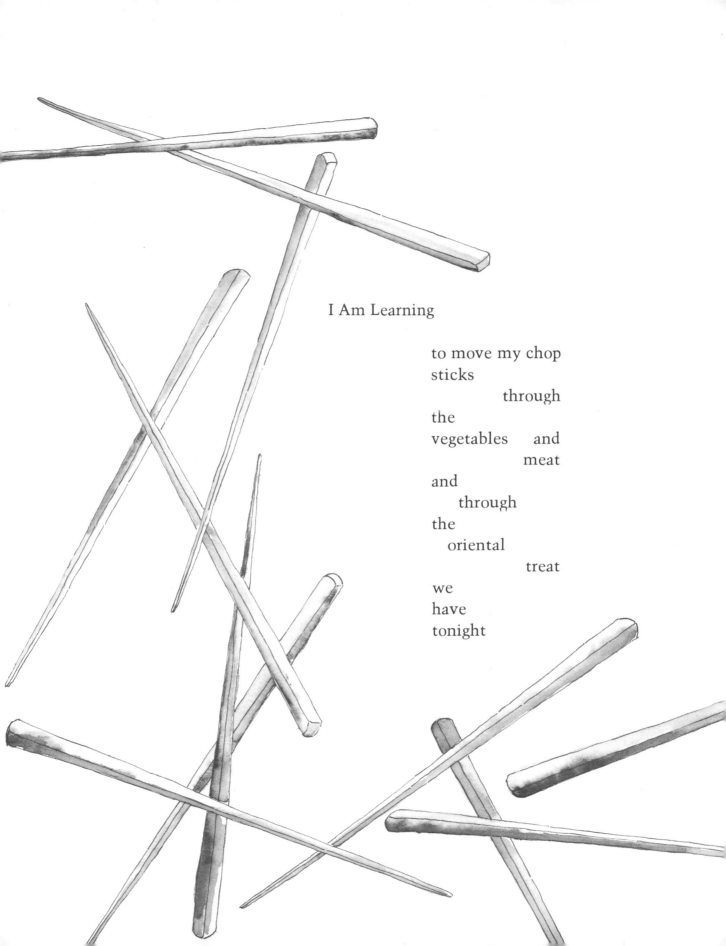

I Am Learning

to move my chop
sticks
            through
the
vegetables   and
                meat
and
      through
the
    oriental
                treat
we
have
tonight

but   in
between
     my
      smiles
    and
      bites
i
write
a
message
      in
       the
sweet
      and
sour
pork

i
need
a
 fork

Deep Into Winter

                                     before the January thaw
when the snow
                        is a foot high   in our field
                        and crusted   with thick ice
and
the berries are gone from the buckthorn
                                        and wild rose

the rabbits begin to eat the bark of young   trees
          the yellow apple   the korean cherry bushes
                            and even the redbud saplings
leaving long tooth circles around their trunks

stopping to chew and listen
                                    their famous ears
                                    are straight up
their noses   point to the safety of the hedge

their eyes in our direction

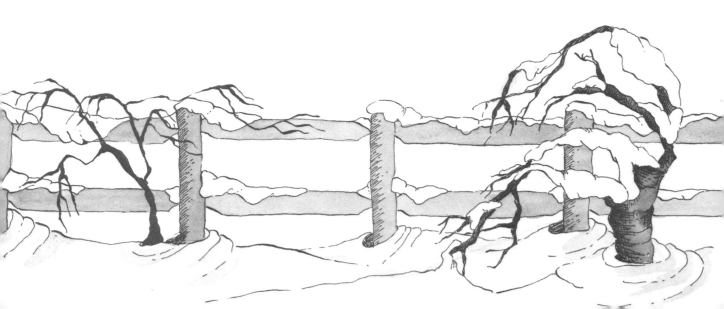

Just

       when winter spreads out
       across the fields   and it is colder
than   we remember cold

here
come   tangerines   rolling up from Florida
onto   the market shelves
                an orange army

almost
       by themselves
they
      are
      the
        seeds of spring

There Is A Place

on
the couch
      for
      grandma
and
a place on
      grandma
for
  me

  in front
of
the
  fire
    and pop
      ping
      corn

The Coach Said

                i had
                    the
youngest
roundest
            belly
he
had ever felt

was
   un
nec
   ess
   ary

        for basketball

The New Pants

                     i found
undcr the
             christmas
                   tree
two
  weeks
ago

are hardly worn
but
      split on me
              yesterday
as
i caught the long bomb
and was trying
              to
              go
all
the
way

I Love To Eat   I Love To Eat
           What

and
i love to eat   a lot
     of all
     of that
        but
i am
     growing tall
        not
         fat
and my
    eyes are almost to the shelf
     my hands can reach
             for
            the
   extra treats each
          after
        noon

soon
   i will be grown